The storm goes away. The rain stops. The floodwater drains away from Follifoot Farm.

The farmer goes to look for his animals. He sees his cows by the wall in the field. They are wet and miserable.

He sees his sheep under the tree at the bottom of the hill. They are wet and miserable.

He leads the sheep and the cows down the track to the farmyard. The cows and the sheep go into the barn.

Oh no! The pigs are still in the barn. The sheep are afraid of them. They start to panic. 'Baa, baa.'

The big pig pushes two cows into a corner. 'Moo, moo ... oo ... oo.' The farmer has to come to sort out his animals.

The farmer picks up each little pig and he puts it back in the pigpen. Mum goes in the pigpen too.

Then he pushes the big pig back into the pigpen with two sticks. The cows and the sheep can now settle down to eat and sleep.